CODE YOUR OWN
SPACE ADVENTURE

CODE WITH MAJOR KATE AND SAVE PLANET ZYSKINAR

By Max Wainewright

Quarto
Library

Quarto is the authority on a wide range of topics.

Quarto educates, entertains and enriches the lives of
our readers—enthusiasts and lovers of hands-on living.

www.quartoknows.com

Author: Max Wainewright
Illustration and design: Henry Smith
Designer: Adrian Morris
Editor: Claudia Martin

This library edition published in 2017 by Quarto Library.,
Part of The Quarto Group
6 Orchard, Lake Forest, CA 92630

Distributed in the United States and Canada by
Lerner Publisher Services
241 First Avenue North
Minneapolis, MN 55401 U.S.A.
www.lernerbooks.com

A CIP record for this book is available from the Library of Congress.

ISBN: 978 1 68297 181 9

Printed in China

Scratch is developed by the Lifelong Kindergarten Group at MIT Media Lab.
See: http://scratch.mit.edu

INTERNET SAFETY

Children should be supervised when using the Internet, particularly when using an unfamiliar website for the first time.
The publishers and author cannot be held responsible for the content of the websites referred to in this book.

INFORMATION ON RESOURCES

You can use Scratch on a PC or Mac by opening your web browser
and going to: http://scratch.mit.edu
Then click "Try it out."

There is a very similar website called "Snap," which also works on iPads.
It is available here: http://snap.berkeley.edu/run

If you want to run Scratch without using the web, you can download it from here:
http://scratch.mit.edu/scratch2download/

CONTENTS

USING SCRATCH

In this book, we will use a computer language called Scratch to code our games. It's free to use and easy to learn. Before you set off on your mission with Astronaut Kate, take a few minutes to get to know Scratch.

FINDING SCRATCH

To start using Scratch, open up a web browser and click in the address bar. Type in **scratch.mit.edu** then press **"Return."** Click **Try it out**.

STARTING SCRATCH

To code a computer game, you need to tell your computer exactly what to do. You do this by giving it commands. In Scratch, commands are shown in the form of "code blocks." You build a game by choosing code blocks and then joining them together to create a program.

Your Scratch screen should look like this:

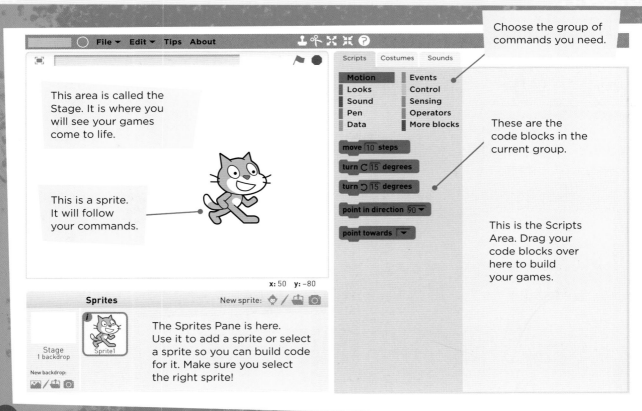

Choose the group of commands you need.

This area is called the Stage. It is where you will see your games come to life.

This is a sprite. It will follow your commands.

These are the code blocks in the current group.

This is the Scripts Area. Drag your code blocks over here to build your games.

The Sprites Pane is here. Use it to add a sprite or select a sprite so you can build code for it. Make sure you select the right sprite!

USING CODE BLOCKS

Before you drag out any code blocks, try clicking on one to make the cat sprite move forward ...

... or rotate 15 degrees.

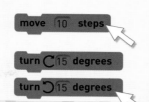

Click in the white boxes (which are shown in this book as colored) then type different numbers to change how far the sprite moves or turns.

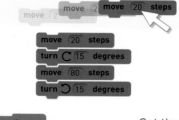

Now try dragging code blocks over to the Scripts Area and joining them together. Click on one of the blocks to run the whole program.

You can break code blocks apart, but you need to start with the bottom block if you want to separate them all. To remove a code block, drag it off the Scripts Area.

Use the color of the code blocks to figure out which group you will find the block in. It will also give you a clue about what the code block will do.

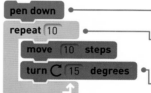

Get the **"Pen down"** block from the green **Pen** group.

The **"Repeat"** block is a mustard color, so it's in the **Control** group.

The blue code blocks are in the **Motion** group.

USING THE DRAWING AREA

To draw a new sprite, click on the **Paint new sprite** button located in the top bar of the **Sprites Pane**.

To draw a backdrop for the Stage, click on the **Stage** button located in the **Sprites Pane** then click on **Paint new backdrop** underneath it.

The **Drawing Area** will appear on the right of your Scratch screen:

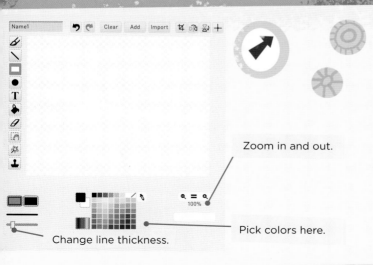

Zoom in and out.

Change line thickness.

Pick colors here.

Brush
Use this tool for drawing.

Rectangle
Draw a rectangle. Hold down the **"Shift"** key to make a square.

Ellipse (Oval)
Draw an ellipse. Hold down the **"Shift"** key to make a circle.

Fill
Fill an area by clicking in it with the mouse.

A call comes in from Mission Control. Major Kate Glenn is in urgent need of your help. Without a moment's hesitation, you race to Mission Control ...

Thank goodness you are here! An SOS has come in from Planet Zyskinar. They have been invaded by a hostile life form. We need to leave right now!

The problem is that my rocket, the Superlooper, is still in need of repairs after an unlucky asteroid strike on my last mission. I was told you had the skills to help.

Can you help me save the Zyskinarians?

You need to get the Superlooper ready for launch. Draw it on your computer screen and make sure that its rocket blasters are fully functioning!

THE SUPERLOOPER

1. Open **Scratch**.

We need to delete the cat sprite. In the **Sprites Pane**, **right click** the **cat**. On a Mac computer, hold the **"Ctrl"** key then **click**.

Click **Delete**.

2. To start drawing the Superlooper, click the **Paint new sprite** button in the **Sprites Pane**.

3. Now you should be able to see the **Drawing Area**.

Choose the **Ellipse tool**.

At the bottom of the screen, click the **Solid ellipse** so we can draw a filled-in shape.

4.   Pick a **dark color** for the rocket fins.

Draw a circle by dragging the mouse. Make it about this size and position in the Drawing Area.

5. Choose a **lighter color**.

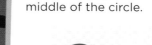

Draw a longer ellipse to be the rocket's body.

6. Drag the body so it is in the middle of the circle.

If things go wrong, click **Undo** and go back a step or two.

7. Click the **Select** tool.

Draw a select box around the left side of your artwork.

Press the **"Delete"** key (or **"Backspace"** on a Mac) to delete the selected area.

8. The basic rocket is now ready.

Change color and use the **Ellipse** tool to add portholes.

9. Add any extra details you want using the **Rectangle** tool.

The Superlooper is now ready!

Turn over to find out how to save your Superlooper design so you can use it for the rest of your adventures. Quick—turn over!

Thank you for fixing the Superlooper! We must leave right now to save the Zyskinarians. It's up to you to blast us off into space. 5 – 4 – 3 – 2 – 1 …

BLAST OFF!

1. Before you do anything else, save the Superlooper rocket sprite you have drawn. This is very important!

In the **Sprites Pane, right click** the Superlooper. On a Mac computer, hold the **"Ctrl"** key and **click**.

duplicate

save to local file

Click **Save to local file**.

Type in **Superlooper** as a name for your sprite. Click **OK**.

2. In the middle of the Scratch screen, click the **Scripts** tab so Scratch is ready for you to add some code to make the rocket move.

Scripts   Costumes

3. Drag these blocks into the **Scripts Area**, in this order. Remember that the color of each block tells us which group it is in. So the **"When green flag clicked"** block is in the **Events** group. The blue blocks are in the **Motion** group. All the purple blocks are in the **Looks** group. The **"Forever"** loop block is in **Control**.

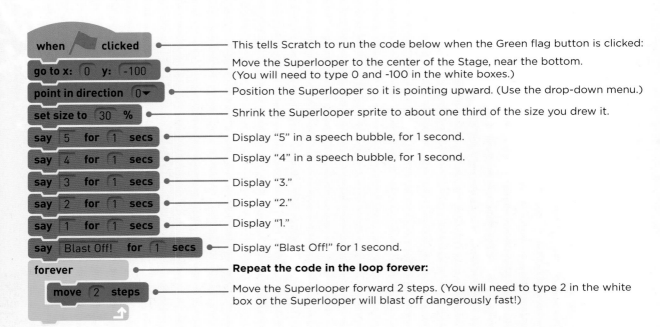

when clicked — This tells Scratch to run the code below when the Green flag button is clicked:

go to x: 0 y: -100 — Move the Superlooper to the center of the Stage, near the bottom. (You will need to type 0 and -100 in the white boxes.)

point in direction 0▾ — Position the Superlooper so it is pointing upward. (Use the drop-down menu.)

set size to 30 % — Shrink the Superlooper sprite to about one third of the size you drew it.

say 5 for 1 secs — Display "5" in a speech bubble, for 1 second.

say 4 for 1 secs — Display "4" in a speech bubble, for 1 second.

say 3 for 1 secs — Display "3."

say 2 for 1 secs — Display "2."

say 1 for 1 secs — Display "1."

say Blast Off! for 1 secs — Display "Blast Off!" for 1 second.

forever — **Repeat the code in the loop forever:**

move 2 steps — Move the Superlooper forward 2 steps. (You will need to type 2 in the white box or the Superlooper will blast off dangerously fast!)

4. Now we need to set the backdrop for the Stage to show the launch pad area.

In the **Sprites Pane**, click the **Stage** icon.

Below this icon, click on **Choose backdrop from library**.

Choose **Slopes**, then click **OK**.

5. Click the **Green flag** button at the top right of the Stage to test your code and launch the Superlooper!

To save your game, click the **File** menu, then **Download to your computer**. When you want to play it again, you can click **File** and **Upload from your computer**.

It is a long journey to Zyskinar. We'll have to take turns piloting the Superlooper. IT'S YOUR TURN NOW!

Take control of the Superlooper. Create code that will make the ship turn to the left and right.

FLY AWAY!

1. Open **Scratch**. Click the **File** menu and **New** to start a new file.

File▼

New

2. We need to delete the cat sprite. In the **Sprites Pane**, **right click** the cat icon. On a Mac computer, hold the **"Ctrl"** key and **click**. Click **Delete**.

duplicate

delete

3. Now we have launched the Superlooper, we need to create a starry sky background.

In the **Sprites Pane**, click the **Stage** icon.

Stage
1 backdrop

Just below, click **Choose backdrop from library**.

Choose **Stars**, then click **OK**.

Backdrop Library

Stars

4. Now you need to upload the Superlooper sprite that you drew earlier. (If you haven't already drawn the Superlooper, turn to page 7 and follow steps 2 to 9 now.)

In the **Sprites Pane**, click **Upload sprite from file**.

My Documents

game.sb2
maze.sb2
Superlooper.sprite2

OK

Find your file and click **OK**.

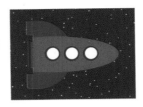

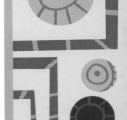

5.

Scripts

Now you need to add code to make the Superlooper fly upward.

In the center of the screen, click the **Scripts** tab. Drag this code into the **Scripts Area**. Remember to look for each block in the code group with the right color.

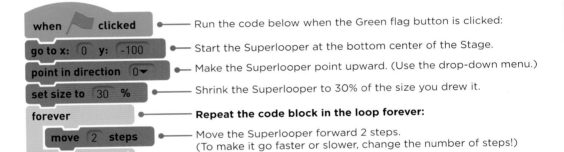

when ⚑ clicked — Run the code below when the Green flag button is clicked:

go to x: 0 y: -100 — Start the Superlooper at the bottom center of the Stage.

point in direction 0▾ — Make the Superlooper point upward. (Use the drop-down menu.)

set size to 30 % — Shrink the Superlooper to 30% of the size you drew it.

forever — **Repeat the code block in the loop forever:**

move 2 steps — Move the Superlooper forward 2 steps.
(To make it go faster or slower, change the number of steps!)

6. Add these two separate blocks of code to make the Superlooper turn left or right when you press the cursor keys on your keyboard.

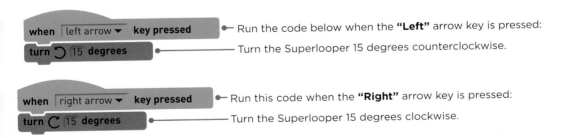

when left arrow ▾ key pressed — Run the code below when the **"Left"** arrow key is pressed:

turn ↺ 15 degrees — Turn the Superlooper 15 degrees counterclockwise.

when right arrow ▾ key pressed — Run this code when the **"Right"** arrow key is pressed:

turn ↻ 15 degrees — Turn the Superlooper 15 degrees clockwise.

7. Click the **Green flag** button at the top right of the Stage to test your code. Practice flying around space to prepare yourself for the next part of your mission.

Click the **File** menu then **Download to your computer** if you want to save this game.

We've hit a radiation field! We must swerve to avoid the dangerous yellow particles or we'll be blown to smithereens!

Quick! You need to create code to make the Superlooper avoid the yellow particles.

RADIATION FIELD

1. Open **Scratch**. Start a new file.

New

2. **Right click** the cat sprite. On a Mac, hold **"Ctrl"** and **click**. Click **Delete**.

duplicate

delete

3. To draw the radiation field, click the **Backdrops** tab.

Scripts | Backdrops

Now you can see the **Drawing Area**. Choose the **Fill** tool.

Choose **black**.

Fill in the background by clicking on it.

4. Now choose the **Brush** tool.

Choose **yellow**.

Make the brush width thicker.

Use the brush to draw in the dangerous yellow particles in the radiation field. Do not add so many dots that the Superlooper will never be able to pass through them.

5. Now you need to upload the Superlooper sprite that you drew earlier. In the **Sprites Pane**, click **Upload sprite from file**. Find your file and click **OK**. (If you haven't already drawn the Superlooper, turn to page 7 and follow steps 2 to 9 now.)

My Documents

game.sb2
maze.sb2
Superlooper.sprite2

OK

6. Let's add a sound effect to play when the rocket hits the radiation field.

Choose the **Sounds** tab.

Click the **Choose sound from library** button.

Scroll down to choose **Space ripple**. Click **OK**.

7.

Click the **Scripts** tab. Add all this code to make the rocket move until it hits a dangerous yellow particle. The **"Touching color"** block is in the **Sensing** group. Drop it into the hole in the **"Repeat until"** loop.

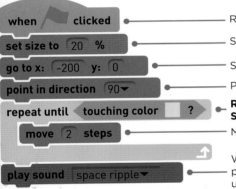

when [flag] clicked — Run the code when the Green flag is clicked:

set size to 20 % — Shrink the Superlooper to 20% of its size.

go to x: -200 y: 0 — Start at the left side of the Stage.

point in direction 90 — Point the Superlooper to the right.

repeat until touching color ? — **Repeat the code in the loop until the Superlooper hits a yellow particle:**

move 2 steps — Move the rocket forward 2 steps.

play sound space ripple — When the Superlooper hits a yellow particle, play a sound effect. (Choose Space ripple using the drop-down menu.)

How to set the color for a "Touching" block

Click the color square.

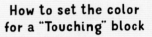
touching color ?

The pointer changes.

On the Stage, click the color you want to check for.

The color is set.

touching color ?

8. Add this code to steer the rocket. See page 11 step 6 for help in understanding how this code works.

when left arrow key pressed
turn ↺ 15 degrees

when right arrow key pressed
turn ↻ 15 degrees

Click the **Green flag** button to steer safely through the radiation field and on to Planet Zyskinar!

Click the **File** menu then **Download to your computer** to save this game.

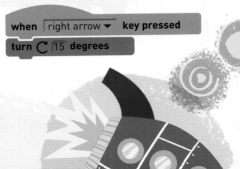

Phew! You made it through the radiation field and are now within two light years of Planet Zyksinar. But Kate has bad news ...

It's one crisis after another! The scanners tell me we are entering an asteroid field. Blast those rocks with the ship's lasers ...

Now figure out how to build code to swerve the Superlooper smoothly out of the way of any oncoming asteroids. And don't forget to code a laser sprite that you can fire at that asteroid sprite.

ASTEROID ATTACK

1. Open **Scratch**. Start a new file.

File▾

New

2. **Right click** the cat sprite. On a Mac, hold **"Ctrl"** and **click**. Click **Delete**.

duplicate

delete

3. Now we will create a starry background.

In the **Sprites Pane**, click the **Stage** icon.

Stage
1 backdrop

Just below, click **Choose backdrop from library**.

Choose **Stars**, then click **OK**.

Backdrop Library

Stars

4. Now you need to upload the Superlooper sprite that you drew earlier. In the **Sprites Pane**, click **Upload sprite from file**. Find your file and click **OK**. (If you haven't already drawn the Superlooper, turn to page 7 and follow steps 2 to 9 now.)

```
My Documents
game.sb2
maze.sb2
Superlooper.sprite2
                        OK
```

5. Click the **Scripts** tab and drag this code over to the **Scripts Area**. Make sure that the **Superlooper** is selected in the **Sprites Pane**. The **"Key pressed?"** blocks are in the **Sensing** group. You will need to drop them into the holes in the **"If then"** loop blocks.

Scripts

```
when [flag] clicked
```
— Run this code when the Green flag button is clicked:

```
go to x: 0 y: 0
```
— Move the Superlooper to the center of the Stage.

```
set size to 35 %
```
— Shrink the Superlooper to 35% of its size.

```
forever
```
Repeat the code in the loop forever:

```
  if key [left arrow] pressed? then
```
If the "Left" cursor key is pressed, run this code:

```
    turn ↺ 5 degrees
```
Turn the Superlooper 5 degrees counterclockwise. (Type 5 into the white box.)

```
  if key [right arrow] pressed? then
```
If the "Right" cursor key is pressed, run this code:

```
    turn ↻ 5 degrees
```
Turn the Superlooper 5 degrees clockwise.

6. Click the **Green flag** button to test your code so far. The Superlooper should turn when you press the arrow keys on your keyboard. The ship will need to be easy to maneuver once the asteroids start coming ...

7. Now we will create a sprite to use as our laser. In the **Sprites Pane**, click the **Choose sprite from library** button.

Click the **Button 1** icon.

Button1

OK Click **OK**.

8. Click the **Scripts** tab and add this code for the laser (Button1) sprite.

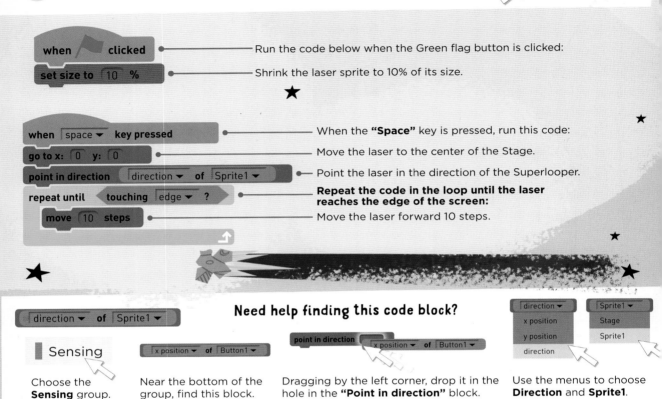

when ⚑ clicked — Run the code below when the Green flag button is clicked:

set size to 10 % — Shrink the laser sprite to 10% of its size.

★

when space ▾ key pressed — When the **"Space"** key is pressed, run this code:

go to x: 0 y: 0 — Move the laser to the center of the Stage.

point in direction [direction ▾ of Sprite1 ▾] — Point the laser in the direction of the Superlooper.

repeat until ⟨touching edge ▾ ?⟩ — **Repeat the code in the loop until the laser reaches the edge of the screen:**

move 10 steps — Move the laser forward 10 steps.

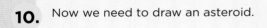

Need help finding this code block?

direction ▾ of Sprite1 ▾

Sensing

Choose the **Sensing** group.

x position ▾ of Button1 ▾

Near the bottom of the group, find this block.

point in direction [x position ▾ of Button1 ▾]

Dragging by the left corner, drop it in the hole in the **"Point in direction"** block.

direction ▾ / x position / y position / direction

Sprite1 ▾ / Stage / Sprite1

Use the menus to choose **Direction** and **Sprite1**.

---

9. Test your code so far. You should still be able to turn the Superlooper left and right. Try pressing the **"Space"** bar on your keyboard to fire the laser.

---

10. Now we need to draw an asteroid.

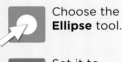 Click the **Paint new sprite** icon.

 50%

Make your asteroid about **half the height** of the Drawing Area. If it is very different from this size, the game won't work properly.

 Choose the **Ellipse** tool.

Set it to solid fill.

Choose a suitable asteroid color.

Draw a circle.

Use the **Eraser** to make craters.

Use the **Eraser** to make the edges rougher.

Use **Undo** if you make a mistake.

11. Let's add a sound effect that will play when the laser hits the asteroid.

New sound:

Click on the **Sounds** tab.

Click **Choose sound from library**.

Scroll down and choose the **Zoop** sound.

Click **OK**.

12. Click the **Scripts** tab and drag this code over to the **Scripts Area** for the asteroid.

Scripts

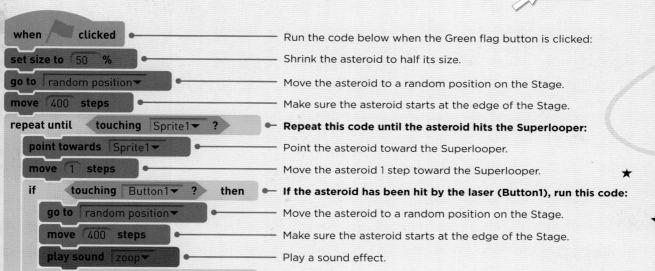

when [🏴] clicked —————————————————— Run the code below when the Green flag button is clicked:

set size to 50 % —————————————————— Shrink the asteroid to half its size.

go to random position▾ —————————————— Move the asteroid to a random position on the Stage.

move 400 steps ————————————————— Make sure the asteroid starts at the edge of the Stage.

repeat until touching Sprite1▾ ? ● **Repeat this code until the asteroid hits the Superlooper:**

　point towards Sprite1▾ —————————— Point the asteroid toward the Superlooper.

　move 1 steps ——————————————— Move the asteroid 1 step toward the Superlooper.

　if touching Button1▾ ? then ● **If the asteroid has been hit by the laser (Button1), run this code:**

　　go to random position▾ —————— Move the asteroid to a random position on the Stage.

　　move 400 steps ——————————— Make sure the asteroid starts at the edge of the Stage.

　　play sound zoop▾ ——————————— Play a sound effect.

stop all▾ —————————————————————— If the asteroid hits the Superlooper, stop all the other code, so the laser stops and the Superlooper can't turn.

13. Press the **Green flag** button to defend the Superlooper against the asteroids. Your game should look like this!

To save your game, choose **File** and **Download to your computer**.

OH NO! Those asteroids bashed holes in the Superlooper. All our food supplies have floated out into space!

I need you to go on a space walk to repair the hull. And don't forget to collect the floating food ...

You need to build code that allows you to collect the bananas that are floating around the Superlooper. You also need to fix the damage to the hull. That's easier than it sounds—you can "fix" the holes by touching them! First of all, draw yourself a space suit and jet pack.

SPACE WALK!

1. Open **Scratch**. Start a new file.

2. **Right click** the cat sprite. On a Mac, hold **"Ctrl"** and **click**.

Click **Delete**.

3. Now we will create a starry background.

In the **Sprites Pane**, click the **Stage** icon.

Just below, click **Choose backdrop from library**.

Choose **Stars**, then click **OK**.

4. Upload your **Superlooper** sprite.

5. In the Scratch **Menu bar**, click the **Grow** button. Now click one or more times on the **Superlooper** on the **Stage**. Make it grow until it is about **half** the width of the Stage.

6. We need to draw your space suit and jet pack.

While drawing, keep in mind that the astronaut sprite needs to be about a **third of the width** of the Drawing Area. If it's much bigger or smaller than this size, the game will not work properly.

33%

In the **Sprites Pane**, click the **Paint new sprite** icon.

Choose the **Rectangle** tool to start with.

Make sure it is set to fill in.

If you make a mistake, just click **Undo**.

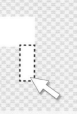

Use three **white** rectangles to draw your space suit.

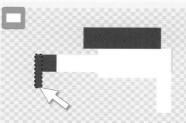

Use **dark gray** to draw your boots and jet pack.

Use **light gray** for your gloves and collar.

Now choose the **Ellipse** tool to draw your helmet.

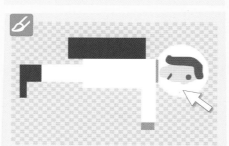

Use the **Brush** tool and pick colors to draw your face inside the helmet.

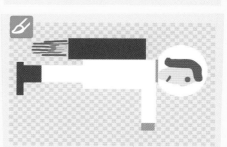

Finally, draw some flames coming from your jet pack.

7. Now click the **Scripts** tab and drag this code to the **Scripts Area** to make the jet pack zoom you around space. Make sure you have the **astronaut** icon selected in the **Sprites Pane**.

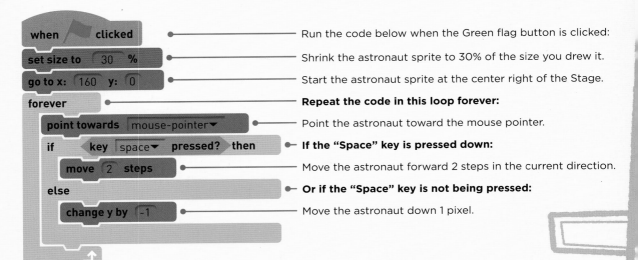

Code	Explanation
when [flag] clicked	Run the code below when the Green flag button is clicked:
set size to 30 %	Shrink the astronaut sprite to 30% of the size you drew it.
go to x: 160 y: 0	Start the astronaut sprite at the center right of the Stage.
forever	**Repeat the code in this loop forever:**
point towards mouse-pointer▾	Point the astronaut toward the mouse pointer.
if key space▾ pressed? then	**If the "Space" key is pressed down:**
move 2 steps	Move the astronaut forward 2 steps in the current direction.
else	**Or if the "Space" key is not being pressed:**
change y by -1	Move the astronaut down 1 pixel.

Click the **Green flag** button to try flying around. Press the **"Space"** bar to fire the jet pack, and use the **mouse** to point where you want to fly.

8. Now we will add the floating food.

In the **Sprites Pane**, click **Choose sprite from library**.

Click the **Bananas** icon.

Bananas

Click **OK**.

OK

9. Click the **Scripts** tab and add this code for the **bananas** sprite.

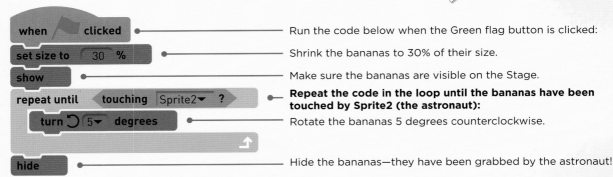

Code	Explanation
when [flag] clicked	Run the code below when the Green flag button is clicked:
set size to 30 %	Shrink the bananas to 30% of their size.
show	Make sure the bananas are visible on the Stage.
repeat until touching Sprite2▾ ?	**Repeat the code in the loop until the bananas have been touched by Sprite2 (the astronaut):**
turn ↺ 5▾ degrees	Rotate the bananas 5 degrees counterclockwise.
hide	Hide the bananas—they have been grabbed by the astronaut!

10. We need to draw the damage to the Superlooper as a new sprite, so click **Paint new sprite**.

Use the **Line** tool to start drawing a damaged section of the Superlooper in **pale gray**.

50%

Make sure you join the lines up. Your shape should be about **half the width** of the Drawing Area.

Use the **Fill** tool to color in the damage shape.

---

11. Click the **Scripts** tab and add this code for the **damage** sprite. To create the sound effect **Computer beeps**, turn to page 17 and follow step 11. The sound effect isn't vital, but it's fun!

Scripts

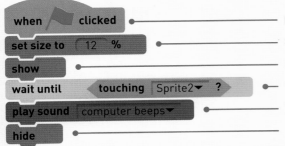

when ⚑ clicked ●————————— Run the code below when the Green flag button is clicked:

set size to 12 % ●————————— Shrink the damage to 12%. (Change if the sprite is too small.)

show ●————————— Make sure the damage sprite is visible.

wait until ⟨ touching Sprite2▾ ? ⟩ ●—— **Wait until the sprite has been touched by the astronaut.**

play sound computer beeps▾ ●————————— Then play a sound effect when the damage is fixed.

hide ●————————— And hide the damage so the Superlooper looks fixed.

---

12. In the Sprites Pane, **right click** the **banana** sprite and choose **Duplicate**. Duplicate three more.

Drag the duplicates around the screen.

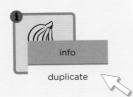

13. **Right click** the **damage** sprite and choose **Duplicate**. Duplicate three more.

Drag the duplicates over the Superlooper rocket.

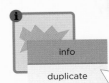

14. Now click the **Green flag** button to collect the bananas and repair the Superlooper!

Save your game by choosing **File** then **Download to your computer**.

At last! You touch down on the barren surface of Planet Zyskinar. You cannot see any Zyskinarians through the porthole, but ...

Planet Zyskinar has been invaded by giant bugs! Zyskinar used to be a beautiful place, covered in fruit trees and flowers. The bugs have eaten everything in sight! The Zyskinarians must be hiding somewhere. We must save the planet! But how?

You wrack your brains to come up with a clever plan. That's it! If the bugs like fruit so much, you can lure them into the Superlooper's cargo hold with those bananas you collected earlier. Make sure you add code to count how many bugs you catch.

GOING BANANAS

1. Start a new Scratch file. **Delete** the **cat sprite**.

2. We will create a background showing the barren surface of Planet Zyskinar.

Click the **Stage** icon.

Just below, click **Choose backdrop from library**.

Choose **Moon**, then click **OK**.

3. We want to fill the Stage with the surface of the planet, so we need to stretch part of the image.

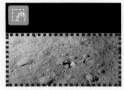

Choose the **Select** tool. Drag a box around the bottom half of the image.

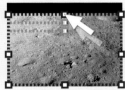

Move your mouse over the handle at the top. Drag it up to stretch the picture.

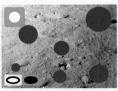

Choose the **Ellipse** tool and set it to solid fill. Draw **brown** craters.

4. Upload your **Superlooper** sprite.

5. Click the **Shrink** button in the **Menu bar**. Now click the **Superlooper** on the Stage to shrink it until it is about the size of one of the craters.

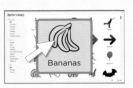

6. To create a banana sprite, click the **Choose sprite from library** button.

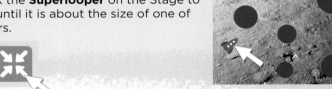

Click the **Bananas** icon.

Click **OK**.

7. We need a way to count how many bugs have been lured away. We will use a special part of our program to do this, called a variable. Variables are a way of storing numbers to keep score.

Sound
Pen
Data

Click the **Data** group.

Make a Variable

Click **Make a variable**.

Variable name: bugs

Call it **bugs**.

Then click **OK**.

8. Now add code for the **bananas** sprite so you can make it follow the mouse around the Stage—and use it to lure the bugs back to your spaceship! The orange blocks are in the **Data** group. The green **"Equals"** block is in the **Operators** group. You will need to drop the little **"Bugs"** block into its left-hand hole.

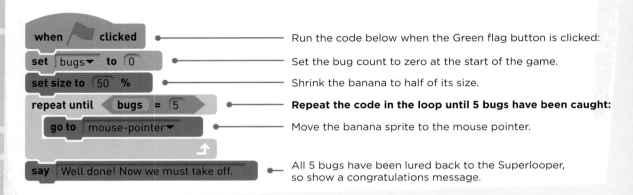

when ⚑ clicked	Run the code below when the Green flag button is clicked:
set bugs▾ to 0	Set the bug count to zero at the start of the game.
set size to 50 %	Shrink the banana to half of its size.
repeat until ⟨ bugs = 5 ⟩	**Repeat the code in the loop until 5 bugs have been caught:**
go to mouse-pointer▾	Move the banana sprite to the mouse pointer.
say Well done! Now we must take off.	All 5 bugs have been lured back to the Superlooper, so show a congratulations message.

9. Now we need to create those hungry giant bugs! Click **Choose sprite from library**.

Click the **Beetle** icon.

Beetle

Click **OK**.

OK

10. Click the **Scripts** tab and add this code to the **bug** to make it follow the banana.

Scripts

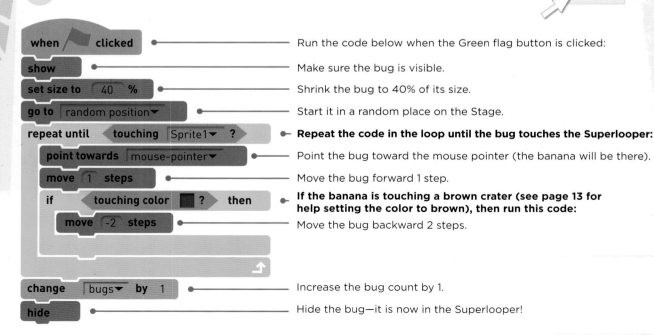

when ⚑ clicked	Run the code below when the Green flag button is clicked:
show	Make sure the bug is visible.
set size to 40 %	Shrink the bug to 40% of its size.
go to random position▾	Start it in a random place on the Stage.
repeat until ⟨ touching Sprite1▾ ? ⟩	**Repeat the code in the loop until the bug touches the Superlooper:**
point towards mouse-pointer▾	Point the bug toward the mouse pointer (the banana will be there).
move 1 steps	Move the bug forward 1 step.
if ⟨ touching color ■ ? ⟩ then	**If the banana is touching a brown crater (see page 13 for help setting the color to brown), then run this code:**
move -2 steps	Move the bug backward 2 steps.
change bugs▾ by 1	Increase the bug count by 1.
hide	Hide the bug—it is now in the Superlooper!

11. We need 4 more bugs to finish off our game.

In the **Sprites Pane**, **right click** the bug. On a Mac, hold **"Ctrl"** and **click**. Click **Duplicate**. Repeat this 3 more times. Drag the bugs around the Stage.

Click the **Green flag** to lure the giant bugs into the Superlooper.

To save your game, click **File** and **Download to your computer**.

The giant bugs are now all safely inside the Superlooper's cargo hold. They waste no time in eating up the remaining bananas!

You set out on foot in search of the Zyskinarians. **Suddenly one pops out of a hole!**

Help! My fellow Zyskinarians are hiding in tunnels deep beneath the ground. They are running out of air. I beg you to rescue them in your spaceship before it is too late.

You must fly the Superlooper through the tunnels to rescue the Zyskinarians. It will be tricky squeezing through those tight gaps. But you must act quickly!

UNDERGROUND RESCUE

1. Start a new Scratch file.

Delete the **cat sprite**.

2. To draw a backdrop showing the Planet Zyskinar and its underground tunnels, click the **Backdrops** tab. Now you should be able to see the **Drawing Area**.

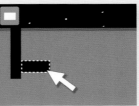

Use the **Fill** tool to color the background **black**, then use a **white Brush** to add stars at the top.

Draw a large **pale brown** rectangle and a thin, **darker** one at the top.

Draw **black** rectangles to create tunnels. Make them roughly the width shown here.

Use the **Brush** tool to add some texture to the ground.

3. **Upload** your **Superlooper** sprite.

4. Let's animate the Superlooper's engine so it looks as if it is blasting. To do this we will create a second "costume" for the Superlooper, showing flames coming from the engine. We will tell Scratch to switch to the second costume when the Superlooper is flying along.

In the center of the Scratch screen, click the **Costumes** tab, then **right click** the **Superlooper** icon. On a Mac, hold **"Ctrl"** and **click**.

The Superlooper sprite now has two costumes.

5. Make sure you have **costume2** selected. On the **Drawing Area**, use the **Brush** tool to draw short flames coming from the engine.

To get a preview of your animation, click on the costume1 icon, then costume2, then costume1 ... It should look as if the flames are flickering.

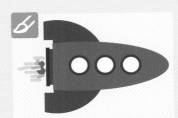

6. Scripts

Click the **Scripts** tab and add this code to the Superlooper to make it fly around.

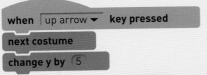

Add these 4 separate sets of code, one for each direction: up, down, left, and right.

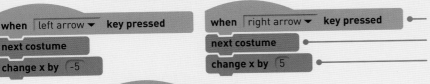

When the **"Right"** arrow key is pressed, run this code:
Show the flames from the engine.
Move the rocket to the right by changing the x co-ordinate.

If you haven't learned about co-ordinates yet, don't worry—this is a good way to find out about them. Just test out what these 4 sets of blocks do!

7. We need to make a variable to count how many Zyskinarians have been saved. Remember: a variable is the way we keep score in a computer program.

Sound		
Pen		
Data		

Click the **Data** group.

Make a Variable

Click **Make a variable**.

Variable name: saved

Call it **saved**.

OK

Then click **OK**.

8. Now click the **Scripts** tab and add this code to the **Superlooper**.

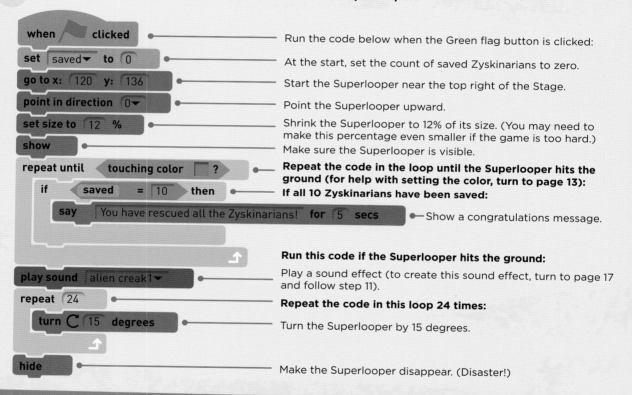

when 🏳 clicked ●————— Run the code below when the Green flag button is clicked:

set saved▼ to 0 ●————— At the start, set the count of saved Zyskinarians to zero.

go to x: 120 y: 136 ●————— Start the Superlooper near the top right of the Stage.

point in direction 0▼ ●————— Point the Superlooper upward.

set size to 12 % ●————— Shrink the Superlooper to 12% of its size. (You may need to make this percentage even smaller if the game is too hard.)

show ●————— Make sure the Superlooper is visible.

repeat until ⟨ touching color ☐ ?⟩ ●————— **Repeat the code in the loop until the Superlooper hits the ground (for help with setting the color, turn to page 13):**

  if ⟨ saved = 10 ⟩ then ●————— **If all 10 Zyskinarians have been saved:**

    say You have rescued all the Zyskinarians! for 5 secs ●——— Show a congratulations message.

↰ **Run this code if the Superlooper hits the ground:**

play sound alien creak1▼ ●————— Play a sound effect (to create this sound effect, turn to page 17 and follow step 11).

repeat 24 ●————— **Repeat the code in this loop 24 times:**

  turn ↻ 15 degrees ●————— Turn the Superlooper by 15 degrees.

↰

hide ●————— Make the Superlooper disappear. (Disaster!)

9. Of course, we need to draw a Zyskinarian sprite! Click the **Paint new sprite** icon.

 50%

Make your Zyskinarian about **half the height** of the Drawing Area.

Use the **Brush** tool.

Make the brush quite thick.

Design your own Zyskinarian.

Use the **Undo** button if you're not happy with what you've drawn.

10. Click the **Shrink** button.
Now **click** the **Zyskinarian** on the **Stage** until it fits inside one of the tunnels.

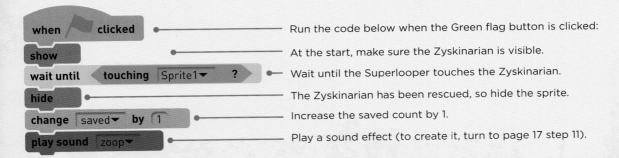

11. Click the **Scripts** tab and add this code to the **Zyskinarian**. Make sure you have your Zyskinarian selected.

Scripts

when 🏳 clicked	Run the code below when the Green flag button is clicked:
show	At the start, make sure the Zyskinarian is visible.
wait until touching Sprite1 ?	Wait until the Superlooper touches the Zyskinarian.
hide	The Zyskinarian has been rescued, so hide the sprite.
change saved by 1	Increase the saved count by 1.
play sound zoop	Play a sound effect (to create it, turn to page 17 step 11).

12. To create 9 more Zyskinarians (there aren't many of them on the planet!), **right click** the **Zyskinarian** icon in the **Sprites Pane**. On a Mac, hold **"Ctrl"** and **click**. Choose **Duplicate**.

Duplicate another 8 so there are 10 altogether.

info

duplicate

Drag the Zyskinarians into their hiding places in the tunnels.

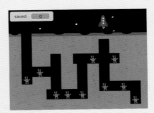

Now race to rescue the Zyskinarians before they run out of air!
To save your game, choose **File** then **Download to your computer**.

THANK YOU!   THANK YOU!   YOU SAVED US!

You still need to get rid of those giant bugs that are munching bananas in the Superlooper's cargo hold. Help Astronaut Kate fly the bugs back to their home world, the planet Bananareeta.

FLIGHT TO BANANAREETA

1. Start a new Scratch file and **delete** the **cat sprite**.

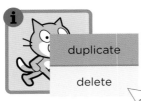

2. Now we will create a background for the Superlooper's takeoff from Planet Zyskinar. Click the **Backdrops** tab. Now you should be able to see the **Drawing Area**.

Use the **Fill** tool to color the background **black**, then use a **white Brush** to add stars.

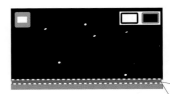

Draw a wide **pale brown** rectangle and a thin, **darker** one at the top.

3. To create the planet Bananareeta, click **Choose sprite from library**.

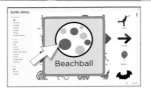

Click the **Beachball** icon.

Click **OK**.

4. Click the **Scripts** tab and add this code to **Bananareeta** (the beachball sprite).

Run this code when the Green flag is clicked:

Keep repeating forever:

Turn the planet by 1 degree.

5. **Upload** your **Superlooper** sprite.

30

6.

Scripts

Click the **Scripts** tab and add this code to the **Superlooper**.

```
when [flag] clicked
go to x: 0 y: -120
set size to 12 %
point in direction 0▼
repeat until < touching Beachball▼ ? >
    move 1 steps
```

Run this code when the Green flag is clicked:

Start the Superlooper at the bottom.

Shrink the Superlooper to 12% of its size.

Make the Superlooper point upward.

Repeat until the Superlooper reaches Bananareeta.

Move the Superlooper 1 step forward.

```
when left arrow ▼ key pressed
turn ↺ 3 degrees
```

Run this code when the **"Left"** arrow key is pressed:

Turn the Superlooper 3 degrees counterclockwise.

```
when right arrow ▼ key pressed
turn ↻ 3 degrees
```

Run this code when the **"Right"** arrow key is pressed:

Turn the Superlooper 3 degrees clockwise.

Click the **Green flag** to fly the Superlooper and its cargo to Bananareeta. Try orbiting the planet before landing.

Thank you! Without your help I could never have saved Planet Zyskinar. Our mission was a great success. It's time to fly home to Earth!

GLOSSARY

Animation – A series of pictures shown one after the other to give the illusion of movement (for example, that a sprite is walking).

Code – A series of instructions or commands.

Command – A word or code block that tells the computer what to do.

Co-ordinates – The position of an object determined by its x (center to right) and y (center to top) values.

Data group – The set of Scratch code blocks that control and access variables.

Degree – The unit measuring the angle that an object turns.

Drawing Area – The part of the right-hand side of the Scratch screen that is used to draw sprites and backgrounds.

Duplicate – A simple way to create a copy of a sprite in Scratch.

Events group – The set of Scratch code blocks that are triggered when particular events happen, such as a key being pressed.

If then – A common form of selection in coding, where command(s) are run if something is true.

Language – A system of commands (in the form of blocks, words, or numbers) that tell a computer how to do things.

Loop – A sequence of code blocks repeated a number of times.

Operators group – The set of Scratch code blocks that deals with calculations and comparing values.

Program – The set of commands that tell a computer how to do something such as play a game.

Scratch – A computer language that uses blocks of code to make a program.

Scripts Area – The part of the right-hand side of the Scratch screen to which code blocks are dragged to create programs.

Sensing group – The set of Scratch code blocks that detect when specific keys are pressed or where the mouse is.

Speed – How fast an object moves forward. In Scratch, we use minus speed values to move objects backward.

Sprite – An object that moves around the screen.

Sprites Pane – Part of the lower left of the Scratch screen where you select a sprite to add code to or change its appearance.

Stage – The area at the top left of the Scratch screen where you can watch your sprites move about.

Variable – A value or piece of information stored by a computer program. In computer games, a variable is commonly used to store the score.

INDEX